Possess the Land: The Believer's Guide to Home Buying

Shakeima Clark Chatman

CHARLESTON, SOUTH CAROLINA

Copyright © 2017 by Shakeima Clark Chatman
All rights reserved.
Printed in the United States of America

ISBN-13: 978-0998611006

Published by Chatman Realty Group, LLC dba The Chatman Group

Unless otherwise stated, Scripture taken from the HOLY BIBLE, NEW LIVING TRANSLATION (NLT), Copyright© 1996, 2004, 2007 by Tyndale House Foundation. Used by permission of Tyndale House Publishers, Inc., Carol Stream, Illinois 60188. All rights reserved. Used by permission.

Also Used: Scripture taken from THE HOLY BIBLE, ENGLISH STANDARD VERSIO ® (ESV): Copyright© 2001 by Crossway, a publishing ministry of Good News Publishers. Used by permission.

Also Used: Scripture taken from the NEW AMERICAN STANDARD BIBLE® (NASB), copyright© 1960, 1962, 1963, 1968, 1971, 1972, 1973, 1975, 1977, 1995 by The Lockman Foundation. Used by permission.

Also Used: Scripture taken from THE HOLY BIBLE, NEW INTERNATIONAL VERSION ® (NIV): Copyright© 1973, 1978, 1984, 2011 by Biblica, Inc.™. Used by permission of Zondervan

Also Used: Scripture taken from the NEW KING JAMES VERSION® (NKJV):. Copyright© 1982 by Thomas Nelson, Inc. Used by permission. All rights reserved

Also Used: Scriptures marked KJV are taken from the KING JAMES VERSION (KJV): KING JAMES VERSION, public domain.

DEDICATION

In memory of my grandmother Edna Singleton. With only a sixth grade education, she was my greatest life professor.

In memory of my grandmother Mattie Tell. The first entrepreneur in my family, she set the example of what you can do with faith and hard work.

My grandmothers' life examples are my inspirations to possess my promised land and strive to leave an inheritance for my children's children.

TABLE OF CONTENTS

INTRODUCTION	1
1. ESCAPING EGYPT	5
2. PREPARING FOR THE JOURNEY	16
3. LIVING THE LAW	25
4. FACING YOUR GIANTS	35
5. PREPARING FOR BATTLE	53
6. POSSESSING THE LAND	59
7. DO NOT DIE IN THE WILDERNESS	75
APPENDIX	78

ACKNOWLEDGMENTS

To the Father, Son and Holy Spirit, thank you choosing me for this assignment and for being my co-author. I thank you for having a plan for my life. A plan not to harm me but to give me a hope and a future; an expected end.

To my husband, Andre Chatman, thank you for being my biggest cheerleader and for always allowing me to be me. I praise God that He chose you specifically for me to share life with and to be my covering.

To my baby girl, Kendyl, thank you for being so understanding of mommy's schedule and for sharing me with others. May God continue to develop your kind heart and giving spirit.

To my parents, Zebedee and Diana Clark, thank you for always believing in me and being my safety net that gives me the courage to leap.

To my siblings, Zebedee Clark, Jr., Nakeia (Niki) Clark, and Horace Martin, thank you for loving me as your big sister. As long as I have, you will never want for anything.

To my village, Tyeisha Sims, Sharmaine Williams, Melody White, Joseph Chatman, Erika Anderson, Samantha Mack, Felicia Stevens and Tatum Hamilton, thank you for allowing me to be in a million places and never worry about Kendyl's care.

To my pastor, Rev. Isaac Holt, Jr. thank you for being a wise shepherd that is not afraid to deliver the unfiltered word to his sheep. Your sermons kept me disciplined and inspired to complete this assignment.

To my spiritual mentor, Rev. Patricia Holmes Reed, thank you for being obedient and delivering the prophetic word from God that planted the seed of this book into my belly

To my spiritual mentor, Ms. Kathy Jackson, I will never be able to repay you for the hours that you spent in prayer with me and for me to ensure that I did not abort my God given assignment. You were an amazing midwife through the birthing process of this book.

To Coach LaVondilyn J. Watson, thank you for always challenging me to stretch beyond my self-imposed limitations and always bringing out talents and abilities that I never knew I had.

To my Mastermind Sisters: Thank you for keeping me accountable and for always challenging me to be the best that I can be.

To my Remnant Warrior Global Sisters: Thank you for warring on my behalf!

INTRODUCTION

See, I have set the land before you; go in and possess the land which the Lord swore to your fathers—to Abraham, Isaac, and Jacob—to give to them and their descendants after them.
Deuteronomy 1:8 NKJV

God gave this commandment to the Children of Israel, his chosen people, after they escaped slavery in Egypt in their quest for a better life. They set out on a journey to enter into a land filled with "milk and honey." Note that GOD did not just give them the land and lay it in their laps, but instead He commanded them to GO in and POSSESS the land. Both of these commandments are action words that required them to do something to receive this blessing from God. Just as they were required to take action, God requires us to also work to possess the blessings that He has for us. Clearly, owning property is one of these blessings. We are the seed that is referenced in the scripture. As descents of Abraham, Isaac and Jacob, the promise made thousands of years ago still applies to us today.

But if God has made us this promise, why have so many fallen short? Why are people intimidated by the giants that occupy their land? What keeps some stuck in a rut, never moving forward and taking ownership of what was given to them as part of their birth right? The answer is simple: a lack of faith and/or a lack of action.

God gives us His promises, but our faith and action are what are required to manifest blessings in our lives. We can have faith and hope in many things but it is our actions that produce results. For example, you may have faith that you can lose 20 pounds, but unless you take the action to eat healthy, drink plenty of water and exercise, your faith is dead just as the bible tells us in James 2:14 NKJV,

> 14 What does it profit, my brethren, if someone says he has faith but does not have works? Can faith save him? 15 If a brother or sister is naked and destitute of daily food, 16 and one of you says to them, "Depart in peace, be warmed and filled," but you do not give them the things which are needed for the body, what does it profit? 17 Thus also faith by itself, if it does not have works, is dead.

When the Children of Israel started on their journey and became free from the captivity of Egypt they experienced many trials, tribulations and adversity due to their lack of faith, action and often times downright disobedience. The actual journey from Egypt to the land that God had promised them really was only an 11-day journey; however, it took them 40 years of wondering in the wilderness before they actually took possession of the land that God had given them. Even then, not all of them were able to see the Promised Land because their lack of faith and action resulted in them dying in the wilderness.

Did you catch that? What should've taken them 11 days, took them 40 YEARS!!!!! How much time have you wasted on your journey to buying a home? Do you feel like you will inevitably die in your own personal wilderness?

Even after God gave the Israelites a preview of what would be theirs and they saw that it was indeed flowing with milk and honey and its trees bared plenty of fruit, they blew it. Twelve spies were sent out to go in and preview what had been given to them. Of those twelve spies, ten of them came back and focused on the giants that were in the land and not its benefits. They told the entire tribe of Israel that it would be impossible for them to occupy this land. Upon hearing this report, the people of Israel were overwhelmed. Having only heard negativity, they decided to give up. Despite witnessing the miracle that God preformed when he parted the Red Sea to help them escape Pharaoh and his army, despite God feeding and caring for them along their journey when they faced adversity, they thought it made more sense to return to the harsh treatment they received as slaves in Egypt.

We all will encounter giants in our lives. Obstacles that seem to paralyze us from moving forward in a particular direction. Becoming a home owner has its share of giants as well. As a real estate professional helping hundreds of individuals with the process of buying a home, I have witnessed their struggles to break free from the slavery of renting and to conquer the giants that have prohibited them from owning a home, or "possessing their land."

What giants have you encountered on your quest to be a home

owner? The low credit score giant? The lack of down payment giant? Or maybe your giant is just a lack of education on the home buying process. Or perhaps a generational giant--maybe no one in your family, not even your parents were homeowners. Have these giants become overwhelming obstacles that have caused you to give up on the idea of owning a home? Have they surfaced and stood in your way of receiving the promise that God has for your life? Have you decided to give up on your homeownership dream? If you have answered yes to any of these questions, it is time to conquer your giants. The first step you must take is to confront what has stopped you. You cannot conquer what you will not confront.

In this book, you will gain the knowledge required to overcome your fears and limited beliefs and operate in faith as you pursue you goal of buying a home. You will learn to stay on track by understanding boundaries and limitations and living within them so that you can free yourself from the bondage and wilderness of renting. You will confront the giants that have prevented you from moving forward with purchasing a home, and you will develop a strategy to conquer them. Just as the Children of Israel had to take one step at a time on their journey, you too, will have to take possession of your land one step at a time. By following each chapter, you will create a step by step plan to purchase your home.

In Joshua 18:3 ESV, Joshua says to the Children of Israel, "How long will you put off entering to take possession of the land which the LORD, the God of your fathers, has given you?" I pose this same question to you. How much longer will you wait? There is no better time than now. It's time to Possess the Land!!

CHAPTER ONE

ESCAPING EGYPT

So the Egyptians made the Israelites their slaves. They appointed brutal slave drivers over them, hoping to wear them down with crushing labor. They forced them to build the cities of Pithom and Rameses as supply centers for the king. But the more the Egyptians oppressed them, the more the Israelites multiplied and spread, and the more alarmed the Egyptians became. So the Egyptians worked the people of Israel without mercy. They made their lives bitter, forcing them to mix mortar and make bricks and do all the work in the fields. They were ruthless in all their demands.
Exodus 1:11-14 NIV

A fter the death of Joseph, Jacob's beloved son who spared the Egyptians from famine, the Children of Israel multiplied greatly throughout the land of Egypt. The new Pharaoh who knew nothing of Joseph, saw this as a threat because he feared the Israelites would rise up against the Egyptians and defeat them. To prevent this, he enslaved the Israelites and even attempted to stop them from multiplying by ordering every Hebrew boy born in

Egypt to be thrown into the Nile. For over 400 years, the Israelites were slaves to the Egyptians. To get to their promised land they had to be freed from the bondage they experienced in Egypt. Are you also living in bondage? In bondage to renting? Renting confines you and keeps you from the promise that God made to you in Deuteronomy 1:8. You are subjected to the harshness of rental increases year after year. You are stripped of your freedom to decorate your property as you desire. You are robbed of the financial benefits that come with owing a home such as tax deductions, value appreciation and home equity lines of credit.

Before you can boldly declare your independence from the bondage of renting and set out on your journey to purchase a home, you must first accept the fact that you have been enslaved and identify the chains that have bound you. Your fears and limited beliefs have your mind in shackles and chains, and they are keeping you stuck in bondage despite the fact that God has promised you something greater: your own land filled with milk and honey.

Chains that May Have you Bound

Your Mind

What has your mind been telling you in regard to owning a home? Is it telling you that you will never be a homeowner because you have ruined your credit beyond repair? Or has your mind told you that no one in your family has ever owned a home, so neither will you? Has your mind told you that you don't make enough money to buy a home and renting is the best you will ever do?

The enemy has a crafty way of planting these thoughts in our heads. In 2 Corinthians 10:5 KJV, the bible calls these crafty thoughts "imaginations" and tells us we must bring [them] into captivity to the obedience of Christ.

Why is your mind, so powerful and paralyzing? It is because every action begins with a thought? You can't do anything without first thinking about it. You can't even brush your teeth without your mind telling you to go to the bathroom and get out your toothbrush and toothpaste. *"For as he thinketh within himself, so is he"* (Proverbs 23:7 NASB) and I will go on further to say as he thinketh so will he do or not do!!

There is a reason the enemy has been attacking your mind by telling you that you will never be a homeowner because you have ruined your credit beyond repair. A reason it has told you that no one in your family has ever owned a home so neither will you. And told you that you don't make enough money to buy a home and renting is the best you will ever do. The reason the enemy has wreaked havoc in your mind is because he knows that if he can control your mind, he can control your actions. Like a puppet on a string, he can manipulate what you will or won't do with a single thought. But praise God, you don't have to be the devil's play toy because we have the power to overcome our minds.

Romans 12:2 NKJV tells us *"And do not be conformed to this world, but be transformed by the renewing of your mind, so that you may prove what the will of God is, that which is good and acceptable and perfect."* God's will for you was declared thousands of years ago as descendants of Abraham, Isaac and Jacob. Here are the steps that you must take in order to take captive of your negative mindset and renew it with positive thoughts that increase your faith and motivate you to action.

Step 1: Take a class or read a book on home ownership. Learn the steps that you must take instead of living in the abyss of the unknown. What you may think is difficult or impossible is easier than you think. You will also dispel the myths that you have about home ownership and will be empowered with truth. *"Then you will know the truth, and the truth will set you free."* (John 8:32)

Step 2: Contact a real estate professional. A real estate professional can advise you of programs in your area for first time home buyers and give you information on what you need to do to qualify for these programs. A real estate professional can also educate you on the home buying process and help you develop a plan to pursue a home purchase. Just as the Israelites were led by Moses out of Egypt, a real estate professional can lead you out of the bondage of renting on the journey towards owning your own home.

Tip: I have built an excellent resource of real estate professionals near you to help you exit the wilderness. Visit www.howtopossesstheland.com to learn more.

Step 3. Consult your Bible for scriptures that you can hold onto throughout your journey. Meditate on the scriptures and hide them in your heart so that when the lies of the enemy enter your mind, you can slay them with the truth of God. The bible describes the Word as a two edged sword. Use the Word to cut out any and every negative thought that is causing you to be stuck in the wilderness of your mind. Here are some of my favorite scriptures that I use in battle to take captive negative thoughts when they try to creep into my mind.

Philippians 4:13

[13] I can do all things through Christ who strengthens me.

Philippians 3:13

[13] No, dear brothers and sisters, I have not achieved it but I focus on this one thing: Forgetting the past and looking forward to what lies ahead

Proverbs 3:5-6 NKJV

[5] Trust in the LORD with all your heart, And lean not on your own understanding; [6] In all your ways acknowledge Him, And He shall direct your paths.

Psalm 37:4-5 NIV

[4] Take delight in the LORD, and he will give you the desires of your heart. [5] Commit your way to the LORD; trust in him and he will do this:

Ephesians 3:20 NKJV

[20] Now to Him who is able to do exceedingly abundantly above all that we ask or think, according to the power that works in us

1 John 5:14-15 NIV

[14] This is the confidence we have in approaching God: that if we ask anything according to his will, he hears us. [15] And if we know that he hears us—whatever we ask—we know that we have what we asked of him.

1 John 5:14-15 NIV

¹⁴ This is the confidence we have in approaching God: that if we ask anything according to his will, he hears us. ¹⁵ And if we know that he hears us—whatever we ask—we know that we have what we asked of him.

Your Fears

Fear is ever present and always with us but we do not have to be held captive to this spirit. In 2 Timothy 1:7, the bible states that "God has not given us a spirit of fear and timidity, but of power, love, and self-discipline". Our fears do not come from God so they must come from the adversary. The very sure fire way to defeat the enemy is to attack him with the Word of God just as Jesus did in the book of Matthew, when the enemy attempted to tempt him as He prayed in the garden of Gethsemane. Each time the enemy tried to tempt Jesus, he gave him a scripture to combat what the enemy was trying to convince him to believe (Matthew 4:1-11 NKJV). We must do the same thing to combat our fears.

The words "Fear Not" and/or "Do not be afraid" appear in the bible over 100 times. The Lord continuously reminds us that we are not to be fearful and to be at peace. In His infinite wisdom, He realized that we will need a Word to combat the fears we face daily. Here are some of my favorite scriptures about fear that you can use when the ugly spirit of fear shows up. (Notice I said WHEN it will show up because inevitably it will along your journey.)

"See, the Lord your God has given you the land. Go up and take possession of it as the Lord, the God of your ancestors, told you. Do not be afraid; do not be discouraged." ~ Deuteronomy 1:21 NIV

POSSESS THE LAND: THE BELIEVER'S GUIDE TO HOME BUYING

'Have I not commanded you? Be strong and courageous. Do not be afraid; do not be discouraged, for the Lord your God will be with you wherever you go.'
~Joshua 1:9 NIV

Peace I leave with you; my peace I give you. I do not give to you as the world gives. Do not let your hearts be troubled and do not be afraid. ~ John 14:27 NIV

When the Children of Israel were finally permitted to leave Egypt after several attempts at convincing Pharaoh to let them go, I'm sure they were filled with fear as well--mainly fear of the unknown. Leaving everything they had known for generations had to be scary. Despite their fears, they gathered their possessions and started on their journey. They had to do it scared.

If you are fearful of the process of buying a home, the greatest way to defeat that fear is know the truth that will cast out your fears and set you free! Here are some common fears that you may experience when you consider buying a home and the truth to eliminate those fears forever.

Fear: I can't afford to buy a home right now.
Truth: With historically low interest rates and increasing rental rates, you can't afford not to buy a home right now.

Fear: I should wait until the real estate market gets better.
Truth: There is never a wrong time to buy the right home.

Fear: I don't have the money for the down payment.
Truth: There are a variety of down payment options available to you including low to no down payment options.

Fear: I can't afford to buy my dream home.
Truth: The best way to get closer to buying your dream home is to buy your first home. The equity you build in your first home can be used as a down payment towards your dream home. You are not going to build equity by renting.

Fear: I don't understand the process of getting approved or buying a home or even know where to start.
Truth: There are a variety of resources and tools to educate you on the process of buying a home

Fear: I don't have perfect credit so no one will approve me for a home loan.
Truth: You can buy a home with less than perfect credit and your credit can be repaired if you are not mortgage ready right now.

Limiting Beliefs

A limiting belief is a false belief that a person acquires as a result of making an incorrect conclusion about something in life. Limiting beliefs are interesting bondages that I have seen first time home buyers remain in. Limiting beliefs keep you bound simply because you do not know something is possible and/or you believe false information. Often these beliefs come from a simple lack of knowledge or just preconceived notions you tell yourself.

One of my past clients who we will call Janine, is probably the greatest example of how a limiting belief can prevent you from possessing your land. Janine was such a delightful person who had achieved a lot in her lifetime and in fact at one point owned a home. Due to life's circumstances and challenges when she came to me for a consultation, she was renting her current residence. When I met her, she had some preconceived notions about her chances of being a homeowner again. She inherently believed that because she was in her 60s, no bank would ever give her a home at her age. I convinced her to come sit with me for the consultation because I knew that what she believed was simply not true. I wanted to hear her concerns face to face. When she came into my office she believed this untruth that she had told herself, but today she can declare the truth from God that she could do ALL things through Christ! Within a week of our face to face meeting, Janine was approved for a home loan!! And not just any loan, she was approved for a 100% financed loan which means she didn't even require a down payment to buy a new home!

In order to overcome limiting beliefs, we simply have to seek the truth. If you have believed you are not capable of owning a home for whatever reason, you have to set out on a mission to find out the truth. In Janine's instance, I helped her to discover that her age was not the limitation that she perceived it to be. You too can seek counsel from a trusted real estate agent. If you don't know an agent, seek references from friends and family members who own a home.

Tip: If you don't know an agent, seek references from friends, family, or coworkers. Seek referral on social media or read agent reviews on websites such as www.realtor.com, www.zillow.com or www.trulia.com.

Contact nonprofit organizations whose missions are centered around economic stability. Go online and search for information but whatever you do, do stay bound in your limiting beliefs. You can begin researching at the following sites:

http://www.knowyouroptions.com/buy/buying-process and
http://www.realtor.com/advice/buy/10-step-guide-to-buying-a-house/.

Just as God did not accept the limiting beliefs that rose up in Moses as he was called to lead the Israelites out of Egypt, God will not accept our limiting beliefs. As Moses questioned in Exodus 3:11 who was he to appear before Pharaoh and lead the people of Israel out of Egypt, God immediately told him that He was with him. In Exodus 4:1-8 when Moses doubted that the Israelites would accept him as their leader, God gave him a sign to show the Children of Israel to convince them. Moses went on to remind God that he was not very good with words, God told him that he would instruct him and give him the words to say and then commanded him to go. God did not allow Moses limited beliefs to be an excuse for him to abandon his mission. So do not allow your limiting beliefs to stop you because God is with you, and He will give you the instructions that you need to possess your promised.

Now that you have accepted the fact that you may have been enslaved to your mind, fears, and limiting beliefs, I hope you find the information in this chapter useful in helping you break free of that bondage. But just like the Children of Israel's journey, escaping Egypt was just the beginning. Let's begin preparing for your journey to your promised land.

Action Steps

1. Take 5 minutes to write down every negative thought, fear and limiting belief about homeownership that you are personally bound to. Ex.: I have bad credit, I don't have any money, I'll never pay off my debts; whatever it may be, write it down.

   _____
   _____
   _____
   _____
   _____

2. Find a scripture that is the exact opposite of that negative thought, fear or limiting belief that you wrote down in action step #1. Write it down or make note of it. Later I will show you how you can use these scriptures in a powerful way.

   _____
   _____
   _____
   _____
   _____

CHAPTER TWO

PREPARING FOR THE JOURNEY

"These are your instructions for eating this meal: Be fully dressed, wear your sandals, and carry your walking stick in your hand. Eat the meal with urgency, for this is the Lord's Passover
Exodus 12:11

In this scripture, God is giving the Children of Israel instructions on how to eat their Passover meal. As you recall, God instructed the Israelites to prepare a Passover meal and to place blood over their door posts to protect them when the death angel came through Egypt. This was the final of the Seven Plagues with which God punished Egypt after the Pharaoh's refusal to free the Israelites. I also find it interesting that as he provided them with instruction for Passover, He also instructed them to begin to make preparations to leave Egypt. He told them to be fully dressed with their shoes on and their walking sticks in their hand, and to eat quickly. They didn't know exactly when they were leaving or where they were going for that matter, but as this scripture points out they were dressed and prepared for the journey which could've taken place at any moment. You too, must be begin preparing for your journey. In this chapter, you will learn how to make the preparations for your home ownership journey.

Determine your "Big Why"

Your reason or your "Big Why" for buying a home is a critical for you to identify as you prepare to take the journey of home ownership. That Why will be the guiding factor in what type of home you are pursing and where you will pursue it. That Why will be the thing you will hold on to when the journey gets a little rocky so it has to be big enough for you to continue on. If your Why is not big enough, you will not complete the work required to possess your land.

Each person's "Big Why" will be different. Some may purchase a home simply for the pride of ownership. Another person may be motivated by financial reasons. Yet another person's reason will be tied to emotional connections related to their family, like my client Harmony. When I first consulted with Harmony, I was immediately moved by her Big Why. Harmony's mother had health concerns that became her Big Why. Harmony had recently lost her father, so caring for her widowed mother was extremely important to her. She wanted to purchase a home so that her mother could visit her and be comfortable. Throughout her search for a home, that guiding factor always came into play as she evaluated each property. Placement of the bedrooms and the bathrooms were important to her because they needed to be convenient for her mother. When she faced obstacles in her journey, and there were a few, she always remembered why she was on this journey in the first place. Harmony found the perfect home that would work for both her and her mother. Recently I learned that Harmony's mother had experienced some other health issues and she is really spending a lot of time at her daughter's home. Isn't it wonderful, that her Why was big enough that she can provide her mother with a space that she can be comfortable in.

Harmony's why was motivated by love and concern for her mother. Dig deep and evaluate your "Why." How will it make you feel to finally become a home owner. What will that do for you and your family? How will that impact your financial and wealth goals? Ask yourself these questions to help you determine your Big Why.

Write the vision

Habakkuk 2:2 ESV tells us to "write the vision and make it plain". Being a visual person and a habitual day dreamer, vision to me means physically being able to see something. Having a vision of your ideal home is an important step in preparing you for your journey.

When I meet with new clients for a buyer consultation even if they are not ready that day to purchase a home, I always ask them very detailed questions about what that ideal home looks like so they can start visualizing it. Often, I begin sending them listings that match their desires so they can begin to see themselves living in the home. It helps them to see what neighborhoods fall within their budget and make plans for what is best for them. It also keeps them motivated to continue on their journey.

What does the vision of your home look like? What size is the home? How many bedrooms does it have? Does it have a big yard? What does the kitchen look like? Just as the Israelites carried a vison of "a land flowing with milk and honey" throughout their journey, create the vision of your promised land to carry throughout your journey.

Tools for the Journey

As the Israelites prepared to leave it is notable that they took possessions with them. They took tools that they would need to help them along the way. (Exodus 12:32, 34). The Egyptians even gave them things. As you prepare for your journey, you will need to take some tools as well.

Scriptural Vision Board. A vision board is a tool used to help clarify, concentrate and maintain focus on a specific life goal. As discussed previously it is important that you keep a vision before you to help you along the way. It sparks the ability within you to dream of what is possible. And *"If you can dream it, you can do."* ~Walt Disney. In addition to adding pictures to your board, add scriptures that will motivate you and declare God's word over your vision. Here are a few scriptures that may excite you about God's promises for you.

"See, I have given you this land. Go in and take possession of the land the Lord swore he would give to your fathers—to Abraham, Isaac and Jacob—and to their descendants after them."
~Deuteronomy 1:8 NIV

"Take delight in the LORD, and he will give you your heart's desires."
~Psalm 37:4

"Keep on asking, and you will receive what you ask for. Keep on seeking, and you will find. Keep on knocking, and the door will be opened to you."
~Matthew 7:7

"And this same God who takes care of me will supply all your needs from his glorious riches, which have been given to us in Christ Jesus."
~Philippians 4:19

"Now unto him that is able to do exceeding abundantly above all that we ask or think, according to the power that worketh in us."
~Ephesians 3:20 KJV

Affirmations/Declarations. Proverbs 18:21 declares that the tongue can bring death or life; those who love to talk will reap the consequences. I think most people understand this scripture enough to stray away from negative talk but how many of you know that you can apply this principle to speaking and giving life to things. You literally can have what you say. Have you ever noticed that when you repeatedly say that you are tired that you get even more tired? That is because your words are producing this outcome. I have learned to become very cognizant of the words that I speak because there is power in our words. The same way you can bridle your tongue not to speak negativity into your life, you can empower your tongue to produce positive results. Even if the very thing that you speak is not true today, your words can cause them to manifest in the future. Romans 4:17 ESV tells us to *"call into existence the things that do not*

POSSESS THE LAND: THE BELIEVER'S GUIDE TO HOME BUYING

exist".

In Chapter 2, your action item was to identify scriptures that combat negative beliefs that you had about home ownership. A powerful tool to speak life into your dream to turn these scriptures into affirmations and declarations. Affirmations and declarations are phrases which you repeat to yourself which describe what you want. Let's take some of the scriptures I listed and turn them into affirmation:

Take delight in the LORD, and he will give you your heart's desires. ~Psalm 37:4

 Affirmation: I take delight in the Lord and he gives me the desires of my heart.

"Keep on asking, and you will receive what you ask for. Keep on seeking, and you will find. Keep on knocking, and the door will be opened to you. ~Matthew 7:7

 Affirmation: I ask and I receive what I ask for. I seek and I find what I seek. I knock and the door is opened to me

See, I have given you this land. Go in and take possession of the land the Lord swore he would give to your fathers—to Abraham, Isaac and Jacob—and to their descendants after them. ~ Deuteronomy 1:8 NIV

 Affirmation: I possess the land that the Lord has given to me as a descent of Abraham, Isaac and Jacob.

Accountability Partners. The Children of Israel did not set out on their journey alone. Moses was chosen to lead them and help them on the journey. You do not have to take your journey alone either. Find an accountability partner. An accountability partner is a person who helps another person keep a commitment. I suggest that the accountability partner that you chose has actually purchased a home since they understand the process and the obstacles you may face; however your accountability partner does not have to be a home owner. It may be someone who is also striving to achieve the same goal. There are some characteristics that you do want to have in an accountability partner. They should have a history of achieving goals. Your accountability partner should be someone that you respect and can accept constructive criticism from. An ideal accountability partner should also have compassion and be encouraging when you experience obstacles and setbacks. Having someone along with you on your journey strengthens your odds of achieving your goal. As stated in Ecclesiastes 4:9, *"two people are better off than one, for they can help each other succeed"*.

Action Steps

1. Take some time to think about your Big Why and write it down. Remember this why has to be big enough to guide your decisions as well as be the thing you hold on to when things get tough._____

   _____

   _____

   _____

   _____

2. Begin to visualize your home. What does the exterior look like? What neighborhood is it in? Home many bedrooms and bathrooms does it have? What color are the walls? How does the kitchen look? What materials are the floors made of? What is the backyard like?

   _____

   _____

   _____

   _____

   _____

3. Now that you have a mental picture of what your ideal home looks like, create a vision board of your ideal home. Display your board somewhere you can see it every day so that you are

constantly motivated to continue on your journey. Share your board with your immediate family so they buy into the vision.

4. Find an accountability partner. Compare that person to the characteristics given in this chapter. Seek God's guidance on finding the right person.

5. Create at least 3 affirmations to combat negative or limiting beliefs that you have about home buying. Post them somewhere you can see them every day. Great places are on a bathroom mirror or a wall in your bedroom or office. Each morning speak these declarations. It's important that you don't just read them but you actually verbalize them since there is power in your words.

_____

_____

_____

_____

_____

_____

_____

_____

_____

CHAPTER THREE

LIVING THE LAW

Put limits for the people around the mountain and tell them, 'Be careful that you do not approach the mountain or touch the foot of it. Whoever touches the mountain is to be put to death.
Exodus 19:12 NIV

The Israelites arrived in the Wilderness two months after leaving Egypt. When they arrived, God immediately set boundaries on them and gave them commandments to live by. Most people are familiar with the Ten Commandments, but in addition to the 10 Commandments they were given over 600 rules and regulations that they were to follow. Now before you panic, there aren't 600 regulations you must adhere to when buying a home, but there are 10 Commandments and some rules and boundaries you must follow.

This chapter will be hard for some readers to digest and can actually cause some to remain trapped in the wilderness going in circles just as the Children of Israel did. If you know the story, you know that the wilderness was not their final destination, but for the Children of Israel, it would end up being their home for 40 years. This happened because they could not adhere to the commandments and rules that were given to them and exercise their faith to possess the land, which God promised.

I often see clients stuck in the wilderness far longer than they have to be. I really saw this destructive pattern in my client, Cindy. When I met Cindy, she was frustrated because she had attempted to buy a home in the past, but had never crossed the finish line by getting the keys to a new home in her hands. She had gone so far as going under contract to buy a home but because of the time and complexity of the sale, she got frustrated and backed out of the contract. As I listened to her share her story, I could clearly hear her passion and desire to own a home so I was confused as to why she wasn't a home owner already. After further questioning and deep diving into what she went through, I learned that after she didn't get her first home in the time she thought she should have, she spent all the money that she had saved to buy a home and also had so damaged her credit score that she no longer qualified for a loan.

Working with me, I helped her find a program that would allow her to build a home while she repaired her credit and rebuilt her savings. As part of her credit repair plan, she was advised to pay down her outstanding credit cards and save funds for closing. She had a clear and straightforward plan to get her the home that she desired not only for her but for her two children. While her home was being built, she documented the process through photographs. She delighted in the fun that comes with new construction like picking out flooring, kitchen cabinets and countertop colors. She knew what she wanted and she was well on her way of getting it. As time drew closer for her to close on the home, as a part of her credit repair program, her counselor checked in with her on the progress she had made with credit repair. Here is where she ran into problems. Although she had been advised to pay down her credit debts, she had done the exact opposite and actually added debt to her credit cards. She knew in order to improve her credit score her credit debts had to be eliminated, but she still continued to purchase items on her credit card. She did not conform to the boundaries and limitations that were given to her.

As a result she ended up losing the home that she was so excited to build because she could not qualify for the loan when the home was completed. When I discovered what she had done, I had to ask her what did she purchase that was so important that it was worth her giving up the home that she so desired for herself and her children. She couldn't even remember exactly what she had bought. For the second time she was close to getting the home she knew in her heart that God had promised but ended up losing it in the end. I am happy to report that her story did not end this way and that today she is in a beautiful new home that she was able to purchase for her and her children. She did what had to be done to become a homeowner. She paid down her credit cards and saved the money that she needed for her home purchase. Because of her obedience, she is in that home today and now has a goal of purchasing a rental property.

Now before you start criticizing Cindy, I want you to ask yourself, has your inability to stay within, or even recognize, the boundaries or the laws you must adhere to prevented you from owning a home? Have you dipped into your home savings fund to buy a new pair of shoes? Or maybe you've neglected to pay your bills on time and used the funds to go on a vacation instead. Have you maxed out your credit cards to buy something you just had to have in an impulsive moment? Each time you do these things, you are prolonging your stay in the wilderness of renting. In this chapter, I will give you some laws and boundaries that you must adhere to get you well on your way to your promised land.

Establishing a Budget

Exodus 19:12 speaks of the physical boundaries the Israelites were given. In the home ownership journey, you will need to place financial boundaries around yourself. These boundaries are better known as a budget. A budget is a plan used to decide the amount of money that can be spent and how it will be spent.

The purpose of a budget is to make sure you have enough money for the things that you need and want. Your budget will help you prepare for future expenses you will incur as a home owner. A budget will also help you identify areas where you need to eliminate expenses or help you identify how quickly you can save for a new home. To prepare a budget follow these steps:

Step 1. Identify your sources of income. I recommend tracking your gross income, which is your income before taxes or deductions have been taken out of your paycheck. You should also note your deductions which can include taxes, insurance payments, and 401k or IRA contributions. As you review your budget you may need to adjust some of your deductions to allocate more of your income for you expenses. In addition to income from your job, you should also include any child support or alimony that you're receiving on a consistent basis. Since overtime is not guaranteed income, do not include it as your budget will be used as a spending plan and you can't plan for something that you don't receive consistently.

Step 2. Track your expenses. This is probably the hardest step in the process for most people because they are not efficiently tracking expenses. If you use a credit card, debit card or checks to pay your expenses, review your bank accounts.

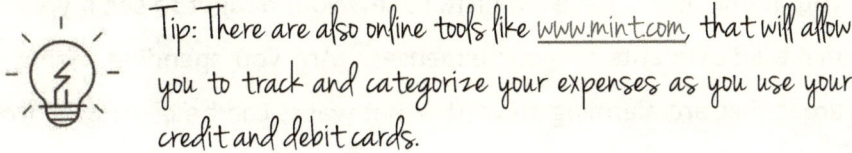

Tip: There are also online tools like www.mint.com, that will allow you to track and categorize your expenses as you use your credit and debit cards.

Cash will be harder to track. If you have lost count of the cash you are spending, I recommend that you create a spending diary for at least two weeks. A spending diary is just documentation of what you spend each day. As you spend money, write down the amount and categorize what you spent the money on.

Expenses can be categorized as fixed expenses and variable expenses. Fixed expenses are expenses that are the same each month. They include things like your car payment, rent and installment loan payments like your student loan. Variable expenses are expenses that vary in amount from month to month like your utility bills, entertainment and groceries.

Step 3. Identify surpluses or deficits. To determine if you have a surplus or deficit in your budget, total you income then total your expenses. Subtract your expenses from your income. If the result is a positive number, congratulations, you have a surplus. If the result is a negative number, unfortunately, you have a deficit in your budget.

Step 4. Create a plan. Whether you have a deficit or a surplus, you need to create a plan for you budget. If you have a surplus create a plan for your surplus that will help you either eliminate debt or save towards your home purchase. Identify which expenses you can eliminate to put money toward decreasing your debt or saving for your home. If you have a deficit, review your budget to see if you can make adjustments to your expenses. Are you spending money in areas that are alarming to you? What wants can be eliminated from your budget? If you have determined that you cannot adjust your expense, you will need to evaluate how you can increase your income. Get a part time job or turn one of your talents into a part time business. Sell belongings that no longer serve you to eliminate debts. These are just a few suggestions to help you overcome your deficit.

The 10 Commandments of Home Buying

In Exodus 20:1-17 God gave the Israelites 10 Commandments to live by. As you go through the home buying process, a successful buyer should commit to following these 10 Commandments.

1. **Thou shalt not change jobs, become self-employed or quit your job.** Maintaining a consistent work history is one the determining factors the lender will evaluate to approve your home loan.

2. **Thou shalt not buy a car, truck or van (or you may be living in it)!** Purchasing a vehicle during your loan process will increase your debt and also add an inquiry to your credit report, therefore putting your loan approval at risk.

3. **Thou shalt not use charge cards excessively or let your accounts fall behind.** The lender can review your credit score as late as the day of closing before clearing you to close on your home. Late payments and increasing your credit utilization ratio can cause your credit score to decrease and can result in your loan application being denied.

4. **Thou shalt not spend money you have set aside for closing.** Before you can take possession of your new home, all funds including your down payment and closing costs must be cleared at the end of the transaction. You cannot not make payments towards closing funds. These costs must be paid in full so they must be available at closing.

5. Thou shalt not omit debts or liabilities from your loan application. Do not lie on your loan application. Your lender will verify your debt and liabilities by reviewing your credit report and consulting databases that will reveal open or default accounts.

6. Thou shalt not buy furniture. Do not purchase furniture on credit until you have closed on your home loan. New credit applications for furniture could decrease your credit score and increase your debt.

7. Thou shalt not originate any inquiries into your credit. 10% of your credit score is calculated based on new credit. Opening new accounts at once presents you as a risk to a lender.

8. Thou shalt not make large deposits without first checking with your loan officer. All funding for your home loan has to be traced back to a source such as your pay check or a gift. Depositing large amounts of cash raises a red flag with your lender and you will have to prove how you obtained the funds. Before making a large deposit, consult with your loan officer to determine the documentation that you will need to source a cash deposit. If you cannot provide that document, it is best that you do not deposit the funds into your account.

9. Thou shalt not change bank accounts. Most lenders will require that you provide two months' worth of bank statements with your loan application. Switching back accounts will delay your loan process since you will need two months to accumulate statements. This could result in you losing your home if you do no close in the time stipulated in your contract.

10. Thou shalt not co-sign a loan for anyone. Although you may make an agreement that the other borrower will make the payments on the loan, the lender will still include it in your debt to income ratio since you are responsible for the payments if the other borrower defaults.

Which commandment do you think will be the most challenging for you?

_____
_____

Which commandment(s) came as a surprise to you?

_____
_____

How do you think disobedience plays into the idea of possessing the land?

_____
_____

Action Steps

1. Complete a Budget. See Appendix A for a sample budget.
2. Answer the following questions:

    Do you have a surplus or a deficit?_____
    _____

    What expenses on your budget can you eliminate or decrease?_____
    _____

    Do you need to generate additional income?_____
    _____

    Based on your budget how much money can you save each month towards your home purchase?_____
    _____

3. If you don't have enough income to save or reduce debt, get a second job, start an at home business, or sell items that you create funds to reduce debt and or save for you home purchase.
4. Once you have created your budget and established a plan for your deficit or surplus, find an accountability partner and share your plan with them.
5. Follow the 10 Commandments of Home Buying

CHAPTER FOUR

FACING YOUR GIANTS

And they brought up an evil report of the land which they had searched unto the children of Israel, saying, The land, through which we have gone to search it, is a land that eateth up the inhabitants thereof; and all the people that we saw in it are men of a great stature. And there we saw the giants, the sons of Anak, which come of the giants: and we were in our own sight as grasshoppers, and so we were in their sight.
Numbers 13:32-33 KJV

After escaping Egypt, the Children of Israel were now free to possess the land that God had promised them. They were on their way to the land filled with milk and honey. Before moving forward, they wanted to know what they were getting into so, as I explained before, they sent a group of twelve spies, one for each of the tribes of Israel, on a forty day covert mission to scout out the land that they were destined to own. Here, they were confronted with bad news. While all of the spies saw how rich the land was, eleven of the twelve focused on the giants that occupied the land to the point that they forgot about the goodness of the land and the promise that God made. They were so fearful that they refused to take possession of their God given land. Faced with an obstacle, they decided that they would rather go back to the captivity of Egypt than to fight giants that made them feel a small as grasshoppers.

Caleb from the tribe of Judah was the lone spy that was not intimidated by what he saw. He acknowledged that there were giants, but he was willing to fight them. He quieted the others and stopped them from speaking negatively and instead declared that they would be victorious. I must point out that the tribe of Judah where Caleb was from means "praise". Caleb was not overwhelmed by what they had to face but instead spoke up and was ready to take action. Coming from a tribe of praise, I have to believe that He knew His God was mightier than any giant. Despite what he saw, this "praiser" focused on the positive and not the negative. We all can take a page from Caleb's book.

The other eleven Israelites' response reminds me of how I reacted to the bad news that I received in my own journey to homeownership. I was married straight out of college at twenty-two years old. Within four years, I found myself divorced, heartbroken, and financially irresponsible. To numb the pain of the loss I felt from my failed marriage, I would spend everything that I made on clothes, and entertainment. I would charge up my credit cards and then wouldn't pay the bill. My only concerns were buying things that I thought would make me feel better or partying, so I wouldn't feel the pain of my divorce.

A few years later, when I finally healed from the disappointment of my divorce, I was back on track financially. Working two jobs to pay off debt, I was ready to pursue home ownership much like the Israelites were prepared to conquer their land until they received their bad report. I will never forget the day that I got my bad report. I was sitting in a first time home buyer's class and the excitement of finally accomplishing the goal of buying a home was euphoric. As the presenters discussed all the benefits of owning I felt just like the spies scoping out the land and seeing the riches that it contained. And then my personal giant became apparent. In the class, I was given the opportunity to speak with a loan officer to begin the process of being approved for a home loan. Nervously, I answered the loan officer's questions about my income and assets and then gave my social security number to run my credit report only to be snapped out of my euphoric state into reality. Although the loan officer said a lot of things, 478 is all I recalled from the conversation.

Yes, 478 was my credit score. Now if you know anything about credit scores, you know they range from 300 – 850. My score was at the bottom of the barrel. The years of my financial irresponsibility had caught up to me. Upon hearing this news, I gave up my dream of owning a home instantly. For about 6 months I threw myself a pity party that no one RSVP'd to. After feeling sorry for myself, I got up from my misery and decided to do something about my situation. Like Caleb, I was ready to take action and defeat my giant. I began by repairing my credit and saving money for my home purchase. Now here I sit the person that couldn't buy a home, now owning my home over 9 years at the time of the writing of this book, to helping other people purchase homes. That is the God that we serve!

Taking action is exactly what you must do to conquer the giants that have popped up and are occupying your promised land. Bad credit was my giant. What is yours? Is it bad credit? Is it overwhelming debt? Is it lack of or under employment? Whatever that giant is, until you take action to conquer it, it will keep you out of your promised land. In this chapter, I will give you tools and information that you need to conquer three common giants that homeowners face in their home ownership journey.

Credit

To qualify for a home loan, your credit will be taken into consideration. Lenders will review your past credit behaviors to determine if you are a lending risk. To conquer this giant, you must first understand it and how a loan officer utilizes your credit report to qualify you for a home loan.

Accessing Your Credit Report. Knowing what is on your credit report is a maintenance task that you should do on a quarterly basis. Some may choose to turn a blind eye to their credit report and just go about life like it doesn't exist, but you cannot conquer that which you will not confront. Pretending or hoping the problem will just magically disappear does not solve the problem.

Annually you are provided a free credit report which you can order online from annualcreditreport.com or call 1-877-322-8228. You are also entitled to a free report if a company takes an adverse action against you (denying your credit, employment, insurance, etc.) based on your credit report. You're also entitled to one free report a year if you're unemployed and plan to look for a job within 60 days; if you're on welfare; or if your report is inaccurate because of fraud, including identity theft.

Retrieve reports from all three credit bureaus, Experian, Equifax and Transunion, since which bureau creditors report to may vary. For example, the creditor that financed your car loan my only report to Equifax which would result in different credit scores than Experian and Transunion.

Review your report to ensure that everything on the report is correct. According to a 2012 study conducted by the Federal Trade Commission one in five consumers had an inaccuracy on at least one of their credit reports.

Reporting Inaccuracies. If you discover any inaccuracies on your credit report including incorrect personal data, accounts that do not below to you or incorrect reporting of your credit history, you have the right to have it corrected under the Fair Credit Reporting Act.

To have incorrect information corrected on your credit report, contact the credit bureau and the creditor reporting the inaccuracies. Include the following information when reporting an inaccuracies:

- Complete name
- Address
- Telephone number
- Report confirmation number, if available
- Account number for any account you may be disputing

Write a separate letter for each inaccuracy that you are challenging. Include a copy of your credit report with each letter, circling the account number that you are disputing. Send your letter certified mail so you will have a record that it was received. According to the Fair Credit Reporting Act, the credit bureau or creditor has 30 days to investigate an accuracy. If a reported inaccuracy is not proven in 30 days, you can request that the entire account be removed from your credit report. See Appendix B for sample letters for disputing credit inaccuracies.

You can also initiate disputes online with each credit bureau, but I recommend you send a letter to handle disputes. Mailing address for each bureau can be found on their websites:

Equifax

www.equifax.com

Experian
www.experian.com

Transunion
www.transunion.com

Mailing addresses to contact your creditors to initiate a dispute can be found on your credit report.

Credit Scores. When evaluating an application for a home loan, the loan officer will retrieve scores from all three credit bureaus. Each bureau uses a different scoring model so you most likely will have three different scores. Your loan officer will eliminate the low score and the high score and use the score in the middle as your qualifying score. For example, if you Experian score is 599, your Equifax score is

645 and your Transunion score is 630, your qualifying score is 630. Credit score requirements for home loans will vary from lender to lender. Before completing a loan application, make sure you know the lender's minimum score requirements.

You credit score is calculated using crediting models. How exactly the scores are calculated is not public knowledge but your score is weighted using the following percentages:

- **35% - payment history.** The largest majority of your credit score is determined by how you pay your bills. Paying your bills on time will result in a higher credit score. A late payment is reported to the credit bureaus when your bill is 30 days past due. Try to avoid past due payments because they have a lasting impact on your credit score.

- **30% - amount owed.** The second largest majority of your credit score is based on how you utilized your credit debit in relation to the amount of credit extended to you. Mortgage and installment loans (car payments, personal loans, car payments) are calculated based on the amount of the original loan and the remaining balance. Revolving debts such as credit cards are evaluated based on your credit utilization ratio which is calculated by dividing the total balance owed on all open credit card accounts into the sum of the total credit limits for all open credit cards.

- **15% - length of history.** The amount of time that you have held open a credit account is evaluated in this category. The longer the account history the more positively it impacts your credit score, which is why you should try to avoid closing old credit accounts especially if you have a positive payment history. Using old credit cards every six months for small purchases will prevent the creditor from closing the account due to inactivity.

- **10% - inquiries.** Each time you apply for a credit card, car loan, mortgage, etc., an inquiry is added to your credit report. Too many new inquiries can have a negative impact on potential creditors because it can be concluded that you are experiencing financial difficulties or about to over extend yourself if you are actively seeking credit.

Note: According to Fair Isaac Corporation (FICO), credit inquires for mortgage, automobile and student loans that occur more than 30 days prior to scoring have no effect on the credit score. Outside of this 30 day period, mortgage automobile, and student loan credit pulls that occur within any 14 day period are treated as a single inquiry.

- **10% - types of credit used.** Your mix of credit cards, retail accounts, installment loans, finance company accounts and mortgage loans have small impact on your credit score. You do not have to have each type of credit but it is good to have a mix such as one mortgage, one auto loan, a few credit cards and a department store card. Because this is such a small portion of your credit score calculation, it is not recommended that you open unnecessary credit lines; however, if you do not have any revolving debt, I recommend obtaining a secured credit card (see more on secured credit card in the Tips to Improve or Maintain Your Credit Score Section).

Tips to Improve or Maintain Your Credit Score

- **Pay your bills on time each month.** Before you are 30 days late, contact your creditors to make payment arrangements or see if you qualify for a deferred payment. Set up auto draft payments through your checking account to ensure that you pay your bills on time. If you are having problems paying your creditors on time, contact non-profit organizations that can assist you with consolidating your credit. This could result in manageable payments and reduced interest rates. Research organizations, read customer reviews and Better Business Bureau ratings.

- **Use your credit wisely.** Exceeding your credit limits will have a negative impact on your credit score. It is recommended to keep your credit utilization ratio at or below 30%. Actively use your credit cards and pay them off each month to generate reportable activity on your credit report. If you are not actively using your credit cards, your creditors can close your account which will impact your credit history.

- **Do not open unnecessary accounts.** Saving 15% at a department store by opening a new account may not be worth what it will cost you in insurance or interest rates due to a lower credit score because you have too many inquiries on your report. While you need to maintain a variety of the types of credit (installment debt, revolving debt, mortgage, etc.), having too many credit cards can create temptation for you to get into too much debt which will be viewed as a risk for lenders. Maintaining three to five credit cards is recommended.

- **Get a secured Credit Card.** If you do not have any credit cards, obtain a secured credit card. A secured credit card is a credit card that is secured by a deposit. Secured credit cards can build positive credit because you will add a tradeline to your credit report which will help with your credit history and it will add another type of credit to your file. When obtaining a secured card, find one that reports to all three credit bureaus so you are building positive credit across the board. Just as with a regular credit card, you want to keep your credit utilization ratio below 30 %.

- **Review your credit report often.** Review your credit report on a quarterly bases to ensure that you do not become a victim of identity theft or erroneous credit errors. It is easier to have a negative item removed from your credit report if you catch it early. Also consider utilizing credit monitoring services that alert you when changes or inquiries have been made on your credit report.

Seeking Professional Help. Managing damaged credit can become an overwhelming task if you do not have the correct information, resources and/or time to do your own credit repair. There are reputable companies and nonprofit organizations that can assist you with repairing your credit; however, buyer beware. Research companies and/or organizations with whom you are considering working. Read online reviews to see how previous customers and clients rate these organizations and companies. A mortgage lender and/or a real estate professional can also refer companies and organizations with whom they have had success. Beware of companies that make claims that they can remove all negative items from your credit report or who promise to give you a new credit file.

Down Payment

Securing a down payment, the initial amount required at the time of a home purchase can be a scary thought for some. Myths about this giant can cause some to shrink back and retreat to the bondage of renting. You may have heard that you are required to put down a minimum of 20% of the home purchase price to obtain a mortgage. Having a 20% down payment would cost you less in the long term of the loan because you would be financing less which means you would pay less interest over the lifetime of the loan; however, it is not the only option for obtaining a home loan. The amount required for a down payment will vary depending on the type of mortgage loan that you obtain.

Down Payment Options. FHA loans are a popular loan product that is insured by Federal Housing Administration. First time home buyers often obtain FHA loans because they have a lower down payment requirement, 3.5% of the purchase price. FHA loans have a lower credit score requirement than a conventional loan, which also contributes to its popularity.

There are conventional loan products insured by Fannie Mae and Freddie Mac that require as little as 3% of the purchase price down payment. These loan products usually require a higher credit score and have stricter underwriting guidelines than an FHA loan but can be ideal for a borrower that meets the requirements. FHA loans require a life of the loan fee called mortgage insurance premium (MIP). There is an initial funding fee for the premium and then the fee is paid monthly as part of the mortgage payment.

An FHA borrower pays mortgage insurance premiums to insure the bank that issues the loan is compensated in the event there is default on the loan. At the time of the writing of this book, FHA mortgage insurance premiums remain throughout the life of the loan. Conventional loan products have a similar fee for borrowers paying less than a 20% down payment but instead, of MIP, it is called private mortgage insurance (PMI). With conventional loans, the PMI can be eliminated from the loan once the borrower has achieved 20% equity in the home, unlike the MIP fee that remains for the life of an FHA loan.

There are loans that do not require a down payment at all. A Veterans Affairs Loan (VA Loan) is an example of a loan that does not require the borrower to make a down payment. VA Loans are issued by mortgage lenders and guaranteed by the U.S. Department of Veterans Affairs (VA). To qualify for a VA loan, you must be an active duty service member, a veteran or a surviving spouse. Veterans must have been discharged under conditions other than dishonorable and meet the service requirements. Surviving spouses are eligible if they remain unmarried. For additional requirements Veterans and surviving spouses must meet, contact the VA.

In addition, The United States Department of Agriculture (USDA) provides loans that are 100% financed. Qualified buyers must meet income restrictions and purchase a home in designated rural areas which is determined by USDA.

Debt

Debt to Income Ratios. When applying for a home loan in addition to evaluating your credit, a lender will also review your debt to income (DTI) ratio to determine eligibility and affordability. DTI is the percentage of monthly gross income that goes toward paying debts. They include mortgage loans, student loans, car loans, credit cards, personal loans, child support payments, etc. Lenders will look at both the front ratio and the back ratio.

- **Front end ratio** is a DTI calculation that includes all housing costs (mortgage or rent, private mortgage insurance, HOA fees, etc.)
    For example:
    - You earn $60,000, which is $5,000 per month
    - Your housing costs come to $1,200 per month
    - $1,200 / 6,000 = 0.20, or a front-end ratio of 20 percent

- **Back end ratio** is determined adding up all your debt payments and then dividing that number by your gross monthly income. This will include your housing costs.

For example:

- You still earn $60,000, or $5,000 per month
- You housing costs come to $1,200 per month
- You have a car payment of $300 per month
- You have a small credit card balance with a $25 per month minimum payment
- You have a student loan with a $175 per month minimum payment
- Your monthly debt payments come to $1,700
- $1,700/$5,000 = 0.34, or 34 percent

Ideal ratios will depend on the loan that you wish to obtain. With an FHA loan, the maximum front end ratio is 31% and the maximum back end ratio is 43%. There is no front end requirement for a VA loan and the back end ratio cannot exceed 41%. USDA loans have a maximum front end ratio of 29% and a 41% back end ratio maximum. With VA, FHA and USDA loans, compensating factors including higher credit scores, a larger down payment, accumulated savings and additional requirements set forth by the lender can be considered to exceed ratio limits. Conventional loan ratio are determined by the lender.

Student Loan Debt. Student loan debt is a major debt that can impact your DTI. The average undergraduate student borrower is facing $30,100 in loans, according to a report from The Institute of College Access and Success released in October 2016. Lenders determine your student loan debt payment one of two ways. If you are actively paying your student loans and a monthly student loan payment is on your credit report they will use that payment amount. If your loan is deferred or in forbearance your monthly payment is still included. In this case if there isn't a payment on the credit report, the lender will use 1%-2% of the loan balance depending on the loan that you obtain. For example, if you have a student loan balance of $50,000 the loan payment included in your debt calculation will be $500 - $1,000. Exceptions can be made for graduated loan payments and income based repayment plans. Please consult a lender for specific circumstances. Either way, don't give up!

Debt Reduction Strategies. If you have extenuating debt, you will need to employ strategies to reduce your debt before pursuing home ownership. God clearly does not want you to be bound up in debt as he expresses in the following scriptures:

> "Owe nothing to anyone—except for your obligation to love one another. If you love your neighbor, you will fulfill the requirements of God's law."
> ~Romans 13:8

> "Just as the rich rule over the poor, so the borrower is servant to the lender."
> ~Proverbs 22:7

Here are some strategies that you can employ to defeat the giant of debt.

Negotiate repayment. Contact your current lenders to determine if you are eligible for lower interest rates which would allow you to pay off your debts faster as you pay less in interest payments and pay more towards the principle of you loan.

Transfer credit card debt. Transferring your credit card debt to a card that has a lower interest rate would speed up your debt repayment. Credit card companies often offer low introductory to 0% interest rates when you transfer debt to a new credit card. The key when utilizing this strategy is to pay off the debt as quickly as possible; ideally before the introductory rate expires.

Pay more than the monthly payment. By paying more than the monthly payment requires, you eliminate the amount of your money that is attributed to interest. Not only will you pay off your debt faster but you will save a ton of money. For example with a credit card balance of $1,000, a 18% interest rate and a minimum credit card payment of $40 per month, only making the minimum payment, it would take you 32 months to pay off the balance and you will have paid $1,263.60. By just paying an additional $20 per month you would pay the card off in 20 months, an entire year earlier and will save $103 in interest payments. Doubling your payment to $80 per month, you would pay the card off in 14 months and save $147 in interest payments.

Use a debt reduction technique. Debt reduction techniques involve you writing down all of your debt payments and overtime strategically paying over the minimum amount on each card per month except for one debt until you have eliminated the debt. You can make payments either starting with the debt that has the lowest balance or the debt with the highest interest rate. Here is an example of a debt reduction technique.

You have three credit card balances:

Credit Card A

Balance: $500

Interest Rate: 18%

Minimum Payment: $20

Credit Card B

Balance $1000

Interest Rate: 16%

Minimum payment: $40

Credit Card C

Balance: $250

Interest Rate: 15%

Minimum Payment: $10

In total you make $70 per month in monthly credit card debt payments. You have determined that you are going to pay an additional $30 per month towards debt reduction. You will continue making at least the minimum payment on all cards each month.

Using the technique of paying off the card with the highest interest rate first, each month you allocate the additional $30 per month towards Credit Card A making a payment of $50 per month. Once you have paid Credit Card A off, you will now take the $50 that you were paying on that card and allocate it towards Credit Card B making a payment of $90 per month. Once you have paid of Credit Card B you will then start making payments of $100 per month towards Credit Card C until you have eliminated your credit card debt.

Using the technique of paying off the card with the lowest balance first, each month you allocate the additional $30 per month towards Credit Card C making a payment of $40 per month. Once you have paid Credit Card C off, you will now take the $40 that you were paying on that card and allocate it towards Credit Card A making a payment of $60 per month. Once you have paid of Credit Card A, you will then start making payments of $100 towards Credit Card B unit you have eliminated your credit card debt.

Use large sums of money to pay off debt. When you receive large sum of money such as birthday gift funds, refund checks or bonuses at work, allocate those funds to additional debt payments.

Utilize 401k contributions. Reduce the amount of money that you are paying into your 401k to use towards debt reduction. How much of a reduction you make is a personal decision. You may consider this recommendation a debatable suggested based on your personal investment and retirement goals. Seek God and consult with your financial advisor before employing this technique.

Action Steps

1. Visit www.annualcreditreport.com or call 1-877-322-8228 to obtain a copy of your credit report.

2. Review your credit report and contact the credit bureaus and or creditors to dispute errors.

3. Develop a plan to reduce your credit balance for all credit cards that are over a 33% utilization ratio.

4. Get a secured credit card if you do not have enough credit or need to establish positive credit.

5. Contact a credit repair specialist based on the recommendations in this chapter if you become overwhelmed.

6. Develop a debt reduction plan.

7. Open or designate an account dedicated to paying down debt and or saving for your home.

CHAPTER FIVE

PREPARING FOR BATTLE

"Study this Book of Instruction continually. Meditate on it day and night so you will be sure to obey everything written in it. Only then will you prosper and succeed in all you do. 9 This is my command—be strong and courageous! Do not be afraid or discouraged. For the Lord your God is with you wherever you go."
~Joshua 1:8-9

After the death of Moses, Joshua was appointed the new leader of the Children of Israel. He was now responsible for taking the final steps in fulfilling the promise that God had given them to take possession of land the land of milk and honey. Scouting out the land 40 years prior, Joshua was well aware that he was in for a fight but he was prepared for battle.

The people that inhabited the Promised Land, the Anaks, were much bigger and seemingly more powerful than the Israelites. It would seem that the Israelites were doomed to fail. In Joshua 1:8-9, the highlighted Scripture at the beginning of this chapter, Joshua is given a formula for success. By following God's word he would be guaranteed that God would be with Him and he would be victorious in his mission.

Now that you have escaped your Egypt, identified your giants and learned practical tools to defeat them, do not think the enemy, your adversary, is just going to allow you to come into what is yours without a fight. In the book of Joshua, we see that Joshua faced many battles with kings, with armies and at Jericho before finally becoming victorious and, you will have to do the same. It's time to prepare you to go to battle and take what God has already given you.

The Power of Your Praise

In **Chapter 2, Preparing for the Journey**, we discussed the power of the words that come out of your month. You learned to declare truths and placed them in the atmosphere. Just as speaking the word is powerful, so is edifying God with our praises.

When the children of Israel were positioned to take over the city of Jericho in the book of Joshua Chapter 6, it was their praises that tore down the walls of the city giving them victory. Out of fear of the Israelites, the gates of Jericho were tightly shut preventing anyone from leaving or coming in. The Lord assured Joshua that he had given the Israelites the town of Jericho and instructed them to silently march around the city once a day for six days as seven priests marched ahead of the tribe blowing Ram's horns. On the seventh day, the Israelites silently marched around the town seven times with the priest blowing their horns. After the seventh time around the city, the priests blew a long a blast of the horn signaling the Israelites to give a loud shout resulting in Jericho's walls falling down. The sound of their loud praises was the key to their victory!

Continue to praise God throughout your journey. If you want to ensure that God is with you as you go to battle, invite Him in with your praises. God inhabits the presence of our praises (Psalm 22:3 NKJV). If you are praising the Lord, He will continue to be in the midst of your fight. I don't know about you, but I can't think of anyone better to be in the fight with.

Gearing up for Spiritual Warfare

In the book of Ephesians, chapter 10 verses 11-18, God lays out a full battle plan for us. He identifies our enemy and tells us exactly what we need to do to defeat him.

> 11 Put on all of God's armor so that you will be able to stand firm against all strategies of the devil. 12 For we are not fighting against flesh-and-blood enemies, but against evil rulers and authorities of the unseen world, against mighty powers in this dark world, and against evil spirits in the heavenly places. 13 Therefore, put on every piece of God's armor so you will be able to resist the enemy in the time of evil. Then after the battle you will still be standing firm.
>
> 14 Stand your ground, putting on the belt of truth and the body armor of God's righteousness. 15 For shoes, put on the peace that comes from the Good News so that you will be fully prepared. 16 In addition to all of these, hold up the shield of faith to stop the fiery arrows of the devil. 17 Put on salvation as your helmet, and take the sword of the Spirit, which is the word of God. 18 Pray in the Spirit at all times and on every occasion. Stay alert and be persistent in your prayers for all believers everywhere.

In the past, you may have read books about home buying, attended home buyer's workshops and consulted with professionals, yet you have not achieved your dream of home ownership. Using these carnal weapons in a spiritual battle has caused you to feel discouraged and defeated.

The scripture makes it very clear that we have an adversary. John 10:10 tells us that *"the thief's purpose is to steal and kill and destroy"*. The only way something can be stolen from you, is that it has to belong to you in the first place. But we don't have to be dismayed because the second part of the scripture tells us that God's *"purpose is to give us a rich and satisfying life"*.

Leslie and Curt Simpson, were a couple that taught me that we must be truly were prepared spiritually to claim the land that God has promised us. I met Mrs. Simpson at a home buyer's workshop that I taught at my church. She stood out to me because she was loaded with questions. Having been a home owner before, she was in the class to learn how the process had changed since her first purchase.

When I met with her for our initial consultation, she came with a complete detailed list of what she wanted and needed in a home. Her vision for her home was very clear and specific. So much so, I wasn't sure I would be able to find what she had laid out. Miraculously, the couple found their ideal home quickly. To be sure this was what God had for them, her trusted prayer partner lead us in prayer in the house prior to making an offer.

Their offer was accepted with no problems; however, this is when the enemy turned up the heat. There were several problems with their lending process and repairs with the home. It seemed like every time we conquered one problem, another popped up. Curt and Leslie were extremely frustrated and downright stressed out with their process, but their faith would not allow them to give up. They continued praying and like Joshua did at Jericho, even walked the grounds praying over their home.

As their real estate agent and church sister, I was obligated to be in this fight with them. During their process, I was lead to fast and pray for three days about the Simpson's transaction. After completing my fast, we were victorious. We were finally able to resolve all of the repair issues and after weeks of battling, their home loan was finally fully approved. The confirming factor that God orchestrated it all was the fact that they were given news of their loan approval by a person with the last name Christ. Hallelujah if that wasn't a sign from God I don't know what was. I always love telling that story.

2 Corinthians 10:4 tells us that when we face our adversary we must use God's mighty weapons, not worldly weapons. Preparing in the natural is wise, but when you are faced with obstacles, your God given weapons are what will make you victorious! Become bold in your praises, pray without ceasing and stay girded up in the full armor of God!

Action Steps

1. Designate a time to pray about your home ownership journey daily. I like to pray early in the morning. Dedicating the first fruits of your morning is special to GOD. If early in the morning does not work for you, other options are during your lunch break or at night when the rest of your family has gone to bed. The idea is to find time to spend with just you and God where you can share the desires of your heart.
2. Seek God and if led, begin a fast. There are several options you can choose for fasting. You can chose to do a complete fast or a partial fast. If you have dietary restrictions, consider fasting from television or social media. However you chose to fast, it should be a sacrifice.
3. Take the scriptures that you identified in Chapter 3, and turn them into affirmations and declarations. Write or print them out and declare them every day.
4. Praise your way through this battle. Find songs that remind you how mighty you are in God.

    Visit www.howtopossesstheland.com for the Possess the land Playlist for some options.

CHAPTER 6

POSSESSING THE LAND

So Joshua took control of the entire land, just as the Lord had instructed Moses. He gave it to the people of Israel as their special possession, dividing the land among the tribes. So the land finally had rest from war.
Joshua 11:23 (NIV)

Contact a Real Estate Professional

Buying real estate is a complex matter with a lot of moving parts and no two homes or transactions are alike. Just as Joshua and Moses lead the Israelites, you should have someone lead you through this unfamiliar territory. A real estate professional can help you avoid potential pitfalls and help you navigate. They will be responsible for guiding you through the property search, financing, negotiation and transaction processes.

In choosing a real estate professional to work with, you should do your due diligence in finding the best agent for you. This can be accomplished by interviewing several agents and comparing their qualities. Here are few starter questions to ask when considering a real estate professional:

- How much experience do you have?
- Are you full-time or part-time?
- How will you be paid for your services?
- Are you knowledgeable about the area that I'm interested in?
- Do you have recommendations for lenders, home inspectors, attorneys, etc. that I will need to work with?

The term "agency" is used in real estate to help determine what legal responsibilities your real estate professional owes to you and other parties in the transaction. Agency relationships should be established with a formal agreement. How the agent represents you can vary. Real estate professionals are responsible for explaining agency relationships to you and giving you a choice of how you will be represented.

Some states also allow different types of relationships beyond agency relationships. For example, a transaction broker assumes responsibility to facilitate the transaction, rather than represent one side over the other. With this type of relationship, the broker is just facilitating the paperwork.

Even though the laws concerning agency can vary from one state to another, one thing that is constant throughout the United States is the obligations of a REALTOR®. A REALTOR® is a real estate professional who is a member of the NATIONAL ASSOCIATION OF REALTORS® and subscribes to its strict Code of Ethics. An additional question that you should ask when interviewing a real estate professional, is whether or not they are a REALTOR®.

Get Pre-Qualified

It is recommended that you get pre-qualified for a loan before you start viewing homes with the serious intention of buying. The pre-qualification process involves meeting with a lender and authorizing them to examine your current financial situation and credit history.

Documentation that you will need when you consult with a lender will vary but, typically, you'll need to provide documents which show your income, your assets and your debts. These will include, but may not be limited to:

- Thirty days of pay stubs
- Two years of federal tax returns
- Two months' worth of banks statements from your checking, savings
- Quarterly statements from your investment accounts
- Two years of W2s
- Profit and Loss Statements if you are self employed

By getting prequalified before you physically begin your home search, you will be able to determine, what homes fall within your budget, and as a qualified buyer you'll be taken more seriously when you make an offer on a home. You will also be aware of the costs including your down payment and closing costs, which you will be required to pay when you close on the home. See **Chapter 5, Facing Your Giants,** for more information on down payments.

Closing Costs:
You will be required to pay fees for loan processing and other closing costs. These fees must be paid in full at the final settlement, unless you are able to include them in your financing. Typically, a minimum

of 2% - 5% of the purchase prices is calculated for closing costs.

Typical closing costs includes:

- **Discount Points:** The amount you pay for a lower interest rate
- **Origination Points:** A mortgage broker fee
- **Application Fees:** The fees associated with processing your loan request
- **Processing Fee:** Fees for gathering and submitting your loan application
- **Credit Report Fee:** A fee to cover the cost of pulling your credit report
- **Appraisal Fee:** Pays for the independent appraisal of your home
- **Survey Fee:** If a survey is required, the lender will charge you for it
- **Courier Fee:** This fee might be included in the processing fee. Basically, the cost of using couriers to deliver documents
- **Flood Certification Fee:** The cost of determining if your home is located in a flood zone
- **Tax Service Fee:** The cost of verifying your property tax payment was correctly credited
- **Administration Fee:** Charges for underwriting and/or document preparation
- **Wire Transfer Fee:** The cost of wiring funds to an escrow company
- **PMI Application Fee:** If you have to pay private mortgage insurance, this is the fee for processing the paperwork
- **Commitment Fee:** A fee to lock in a rate
- **Inspection Fee:** A charge for any required inspection

The amount of closing costs that you pay can be limited. Closing costs will vary from lender to lender, so ask your lender to give you an estimate of the costs to close, and then comparison shop. When making your offer, you can ask the seller to pay some of the closing costs. Also ask your lender if they can give you credits towards your closing cost or if you qualify for programs that will contribute to paying your closings costs. As its states in James 4:2 KJV, *"you have not because you ask not"*.

Find the Right Home

As we discussed in **Chapter 3, Preparing for the Journey**, you probably already have a vision in mind of what your dream home will look like. Keeping that vision in your head probably kept you motivated throughout the process of defeating the giants that were in your promised land. Now that you are at the point of actually physically searching for a home, you should really prioritize your needs. Notice I said your needs. There will be a lot of things that you want, but your needs should be your priority.

How many bedrooms do you need to accommodate your family? Do you need the home to be in a particular school zone for your children? How close is the home to your work and how will the location impact your daily commute? These are the types of questions you should ask to help determine your needs. While things like a swimming pool in the backyard, hardwood floors and granite countertops are all available to you, you should always keep your needs above things that could be just your wants.

If the perfect home meets your needs, but may be missing a few of your wants, you must "eat the manna". I often tell this to my clients. You should see the look on their faces when I first use that term. What I am telling them is to be grateful for what God has provided. When the Children of Israel were in the Wilderness, God provided manna for them every day. It wasn't the rich food that they had in Egypt and longed for, but it satisfied their need for nourishment. You may not get the grand mansion that you have dreamed of in your first home, but be satisfied that God has provided you the ability to own a home. Do not dishonor Him or show that you are ungrateful by not being satisfied by what He has provided.

Keeping in line with the journey, the Children of Israel complained so much about manna that God finally gave in and gave them quail to eat. When they gathered and ate the quail they were struck with a plague and several of them died. Take a lesson from the Israelites. Don't bite off more than you can chew by getting into a home that you won't be able to physically or financially manage. The gift that God gives you will not bring you sorrow (Proverbs 10:22).

Almost 90% of buyers use the Internet to search for homes. Consult with your real estate professional about the best place to search for homes online for accurate data. Keep your agent informed of properties that you are interested in and make time in your schedule to view homes in person. While their property details may seem similar online, homes can actually be very different in terms of layout, design, workmanship and other aspects that you will only find out when viewing them in person. In addition, you should view homes with the help of your real estate professional. They will have the knowledge and experience to advise you on things you should be looking at in the home. They can also provide you with market data for the neighborhood.

Make an Offer

Once you have found your dream home, you are ready to present an offer to the seller. Your real estate professional will help you put the written offer together on a contract. The offer will include many details but not limited to, the amount you are willing to pay for the property, when the property will close, the responsibilities of the buyer and seller in the transaction and contingencies to name a few.

Contingencies are provisions for unforeseen events or circumstance. Examples of contingencies in your offer can include your satisfaction with the home inspection, your loan being successfully approved, the seller making adjustments to the home prior to closing to name a few. Your real estate professional will guide you through writing an offer and advise about the appropriate contingencies.

Your offer will include an earnest deposit. This is a cash deposit you make when putting in your written offer on a property to show your "good faith". The amount of the earnest money is usually about .5% to 1% of the purchase price but the prices is a negotiable item in the offer. The funds are held by a real estate agency or an attorney's office usually holds the deposit, the amount varies by negotiations and help with a designated escrow agent such as a real estate office, title company or attorney. The funds are credited to the buyer at closing and can be refunded to the buyer if the transaction does not go through depending on the language of the contract.

There are instances where the earnest deposit could be forfeited. This usually occurs when the buyer has defaulted on terms of the contract that would enable the seller to keep the earnest deposit. This would require a mutual agreement by the seller and the buyer or a court order in most states.

A buyer can expect there to be some back and forth when submitting an offer. When presenting an offer you tell the seller your desired terms. The seller can choose to counter parts of your offer or reject them outright. Your real estate professional will act as your liaison and facilitate your negotiations. When both the buyer and seller agree on all terms in writing, the contract is considered pending or ratified.

Inspect the Home

Just as the Israelites scoped out and investigated their land, you should also do a thorough investigation of your home in the form of a home inspection. Getting a home inspection should be considered an investment in your purchase. The cost will be determined by the inspection company and will be determined by the size, age and areas the inspector will need to inspect. If you do not know of any inspectors, your real estate professional can assist you in hiring a licensed and bonded inspector to do a thorough inspection of the home including:
- Roof
- Structure
- Exterior
- Electrical system

- Heating and Air Conditioning system
- Plumbing system
- Insulation
- Interior
- Built-In Appliances
- Garage

The inspection is not designed to criticize every minor problem or defect in the home. It is intended to report on major damage or serious problems that require repair. Should serious problems be indicated, the inspector will recommend that a structural engineer or other professional inspect it as well.

I recommend that you are present for the home inspections. You will be able to clearly understand the inspection report, and know exactly which areas need attention. Plus, you can get answers to many questions, tips for maintenance, and a lot of general information that will help you once you move into your new home.

Your home cannot "pass or fail" an inspection, and your inspector will not tell you whether he/she thinks the home is worth the money you are offering. The inspector's job is to make you aware of repairs that are recommended or necessary and provide you with an inspection report. In addition to the overall inspection, you may wish to have separate tests conducted for termites or the presence of radon gas and or lead based paint depending on the age of the home.

From the inspector's report, you can present a list of repairs that you would like the seller to address. Ideally, the seller will complete all the repairs on your list but you may have to negotiate some of the repairs. Part of the negotiations could include the seller giving you a credit to make the repairs yourself after closing. The inspection period can be a contentious time during the purchasing process and one of the outcomes could be that you and the seller do not come to an agreement on the repairs. Depending on the language of your contract, this could result in you terminating the agreement and receiving your earnest deposit back. When presenting your offer, be sure that you understand clearly the terms of your contract as it relates to repair requests.

The best way to approach this sensitive time is with a level head. Take your emotions out of it and use your inspection report to help you come to a conclusion. I've seen clients back out of a deal because they did not "win" the battle of negotiating repairs. Before coming to that conclusion, really ask yourself if you are making a logical decision or an emotional decision. Seek the guidance of your real estate professional who is experienced in dealing these matters. As it's states in Proverbs 11:14 ESV, *"where there is no guidance the people fall, but in an abundance of counselors there is victory."* Between the counsel of your home inspector and your real estate professional, they will assist you in coming to a victorious solution.

Secure Your Loan

Once you have a pending or ratified contract, you will need to inform your lender so they can finalize the details of your application and progress toward closing the loan. At this time, you will finalize the type of loan you will use, your down payment, interest rate, regular payment schedule and any other financial conditions associated with the closing.

By going through the pre-qualification process, you've already provided the lender with a lot of the information that they need so the process should be straightforward. Your loan officer will submit your loan application for processing once they have received all the documents they have requested. A loan processor will then step in to prepare the file for underwriting. An underwriter will review the loan package to determine the buyer's ability to pay off the loan and their credit history. It is not unusual for an underwriter to request additional documentation from the buyer. Once the underwriter has completed their review, the loan will be conditionally approved. The loan officer will advise you of any additional conditions that you must meet to get final loan approval.

During the loan process, your lender will also order an appraisal of the home and request a title search. An appraisal is an expert estimation of the value of a property. An appraiser will be hired for you by the lender. Depending on the lender's policies, you may be required to pay for this appraisal upfront or you will have to pay for it at closing. If you have successfully negotiated seller paid closing costs, the appraisal will be covered by the seller.

Ideally the appraisal will come back at the value or higher than the value for which you have contracted to purchase the property. There is a possibility of a low appraisal where the appraisal comes in lower than the contracted prices. In this instance, you can renegotiate the sales price with the seller if your contract has an appraisal contingency.

If the seller is not willing to lower the price based on the appraisal, depending on your contract language, you can terminate the contract and receive your earnest deposit back. Loans such as FHA loans and VA loans actually include an addendum stating that the property has to appraise at value to be financed. With a conventional loan, you may also proceed with the contract, but you will have to cover the difference of the contract price and the appraisal price as the lender will base the amount of the financing on the appraisal. There are instances where the appraisal can be contested and another appraisal is ordered to resolve the issue.

A title search is performed to ensure the person or persons on the sales contract have the legal right to sell the home. The title search also ensures that there aren't any clouds on the loan which would be any claims, liens or encumbrances against the property. It is the responsibility of the seller to clear up any clouds that pop up and guarantee a clear title.

Once a title search has been completed, I recommend that you obtain title insurance. Title insurance insures against any claims against the title that may come up due to incorrect information provided by the title company. There are two types of title insurance. The first is coverage that protects the lender for the amount of the mortgage. Owner's can elect to purchase the second form of coverage: an owner's policy which protects your equity in the property.

During the time that you securing your loan, you should definitely continue to pray and keep your request before the Lord. Remember the Lord has promised us that if we delight ourselves in him, he will give us the desires of our heart (Psalms 37:4). There are instances where loans can be denied. It is at those times that I have to remind my clients that God has also promised us that he will not withhold any GOOD thing from us (Psalm 84:11). It can be a heartbreaking feeling but know that God always has your best interests at heart.

To ensure that you have a smooth transaction, make sure that you keep yourself mortgage ready. Continue to follow the Ten Commandments of Home Buying that were laid out in **Chapter 3, living the Law.** Before you make large deposits to your bank accounts consult with your loan officer and do not take out any new lines of credit or have your credit pulled for any reason.

The entire lending process will vary from lender to lender but you can expect the process to take between 30 – 60 days. Ask your lender what their standard times are from contract to closing. The length of time that it takes, the number of people involved in the process, the demands for additional documentation and issues that can arise can contribute to making the loan process stressful for a buyer. After you have been thoroughly reviewed through the loan process and the property, you will be issued a clear to close by your lender.

Close the Deal

Following the clear to close from lender, a date will be set to close on the loan. Prior to closing, I recommend that you do a final walk through of the home. During the final walkthrough you'll be given the chance to look at the home to make sure it's in the same condition as when you signed the sales agreement. It is also a time to ensure that repairs that were agreed upon have been completed and all terms and contingencies in the contract related to the condition of the property have been met.

During the closing, the closing agent, will review your settlement statement with you. A settlement statement is a document that gives a breakdown of the costs that the buyer and seller are responsible for on the closing date. The settlement statement is usually provided prior to the closing day. Review the statement with your real estate professional and/or lender to be sure that it is correct.

The settlement statement will also make you aware of the amount of funds that you will need to close on the home. This will include your down payment and closing cost that have not been covered by financing, or lender or seller concessions. You will be instructed to bring a cashier's check or wire the funds to cover the cash that you need to close.

At the closing table you will sign several documents to finalize the conveyance of the property from the seller to you. Once the documents have been reviewed and cleared for funding by the lender, you will receive the keys to your new home!!!!

Dedicate Your Home to God

Achieving the goal of owning a home is a great accomplishment but do not forget who gave it to you. In Deuteronomy 8:10-18, prior to entering their promised land, the Israelites are given a reminder so they did not forget the God.

> 10 When you have eaten your fill, be sure to praise the Lord your God for the good land he has given you. 11 "But that is the time to be careful! Beware that in your plenty you do not forget the Lord your God and disobey his commands, regulations, and decrees that I am giving you today. 12 For when you have become full and prosperous and have built fine homes to live in, 13 and when your flocks and herds have become very large and your silver and gold have multiplied along with everything else, be careful!
>
> 14 Do not become proud at that time and forget the Lord your God, who rescued you from slavery in the land of Egypt. 15 Do not forget that he led you through the great and terrifying wilderness with its poisonous snakes and scorpions, where it was so hot and dry. He gave you water from the rock! 16 He fed you with manna in the wilderness, a food unknown to your ancestors. He did this to humble you and test you for your own good.
>
> 17 He did all this so you would never say to yourself, 'I have achieved this wealth with my own strength and energy.' 18 Remember the Lord your God. He is the one who gives you power to be successful, in order to fulfill the covenant he confirmed to your ancestors with an oath.

This was a warning that Moses gave before he died to remind the Israelites that without God the inheritance would not be possible. Without God, your inheritance would not be possible either. Be sure to give him glory for what you have achieved. Honor him by blessing your home and dedicating it back to Him. Show his love by creating a home that is a safe haven and a mantle of peace for you, your spouse and your children. Welcome your family and friends into your home as you create an atmosphere of love.

Actions Steps

This chapter is a series of action steps. Take the first action step by contacting a real estate professional. Visit our website at www.howtopossesstheland.com for a list of real estate professionals in your area that are part of The Possess the Land Network.

CHAPTER SEVEN

DO NOT DIE IN THE WILDERNESS

This book paralleled the Children of Israel's journey from Egypt to the promised land with the journey of home ownership. The Israelites were a huge family that descended from Abraham, the father of many nations as God promised him, (Genesis 17:4). I hope this family's story and the stories of my clients have inspired you to aggressively move forward with possessing the land that God has promised you. Before I conclude I want to share one final story with you: my family's story.

Growing up as a child I remember being at my grandmother's house for holidays, family barbecues, and parties. It was not an extravagant home, having only two bedrooms and one bathroom compacted into 800 square feet, but it was our gathering space. We could easily squeeze 40-50 folks inside and be comfortable. It was always a place that I associated with happiness. I spent entire summers at my grandmother's house where I felt free to go to exotic destinations in my imagination in her backyard. I still can visualize the tree in the front yard as the Love Boat that my cousins and I imagined taking us on tropical excursions.

Although my grandmother would live in this home over 30 years, she would never own it. If you added up all the rent she paid over three decades, she had essentially paid for the home. She made repairs and improvements to the home at her expense as if it were her own. Despite what she had put into the home, she ended up losing it when her landlord died. The rent increased to an amount that was no longer affordable for my grandmother, which resulted in her having to move. Eventually the house was sold taking away the home that held so many of our wonderful memories. My grandmother would die at age 94 never becoming a home owner.

We no longer had a central location to gather or to call home. Our safe space had been taken away and sold to someone who could never appreciate all the memories that were made there. This made me vow that I would become a home owner. I would have something to leave to my children and my children's children as the bible instructs us (Proverbs 13:22 NIV).

As I discuss in **Chapter 5, Facing Your Giants,** initially when I set out to be a homeowner, I faced a lot of obstacles. My credit was shot from my divorce, and I was struggling financially largely due to my misuse of my resources and not being a good steward over what God had blessed me with. Possessing a 478 credit score, living from pay check to pay check and caught up in the trap of pay day loans, I didn't believe. I could have given up on being a home owner like the generation of the Israelites that were not permitted to see the Promised Land because of their fear of their giants. Their lack of faith caused them to wonder in the wilderness and ultimately die there. That does not have to be your destiny!

Like Caleb, you can put your faith in God and see past the giants. Like Joshua, you can conquer your giants and possess what God has promised you. Just as I went from a 478 credit score, to buying a home where my family can now gather, to selling homes, you can conquer your giants and possess the land that God has given you.

Jeremiah 29:5 states *"Build homes, and plan to stay. Plant gardens, and eat the food they produce."* This is just one of the many promises that God has given you in regard to home ownership and gaining wealth. Stand on those promises. Do not give up! Defeat your Giants! God has given us the authority to overcome each and everyone them. Apply the information and tools in this book and evict the giants that are inhabiting your promised land. Do not die in your personal wilderness.

IT'S TIME TO POSSESS THE LAND.

APPENDIX

APPENDIX A: Budget

Income:

Salary (after deductions) _____

Spouse income (after deductions) _____

Child Support _____

Investment Income _____

Rental Income _____

Other _____

Total Fixed Income _____

Fixed Expenses:

Tithes _____

Regular Savings _____

Rent/Mortgage _____

Vehicle Payments _____

Other Transportation   _____

Credit Card Payments   _____

Personal Loans   _____

Student Loans   _____

Insurance (Life and Health)   _____

Home/Rental Insurance   _____

Auto Insurance   _____

Auto Registration/Taxes   _____

Child Care   _____

Other   _____

Total Fixed Expenses _____

Variable Expenses:

Food/household supplies   _____

Dining Out   _____

POSSESS THE LAND: THE BELIEVER'S GUIDE TO HOME BUYING

Clothes _____

Laundry/dry cleaning _____

Gas, Oil, Auto Maintenance _____

Parking _____

Medical/Dental/Eye Care _____

Entertainment _____

Travel/Vacation _____

Service Animals, Pets, Supplies, Food _____

Music and Books _____

Personal Care _____

Subscriptions _____

Cable TV and Internet _____

Phone _____

Gifts _____

Charity/Contributions _____

Other _____

Total Variable Expenses _____

Total Fixed Expenses _____

Total Monthly Expenses _____

Total Income _____

Less Total Expenses _____

Total Discretionary Income
(or Deficit) _____

APPENDIX B: Credit Repair Letters

Letter Disputing Credit Report

[your name and address]

[name and address of the credit report agency]

[date]

To Whom It May Concern:

Recently I received my credit report from you agency. My file or report number is _____. In reviewing my report, I noticed the following errors (s)"
1._____

This item is incorrect because_____
and should instead indicate_____

2._____

This item is incorrect because_____
and should instead indicate_____

3._____

This item is incorrect because_____
and should instead indicate_____

I would appreciate it if these errors could be corrected. I look forward to hearing from you within thirty days.

Sincerely,

Letter to Creditor Regarding Incorrect Credit Report

[your name and address]

[name and address of the credit report agency]

[date]

To Whom It May Concern:

I am writing to you in regard to my account, number_____.
I recently received a copy of my credit report from the following credit reporting agency(s):_____.

My account with you is incorrectly listed as _____ when in fact it is _____.

I have asked the credit reporting agency to verify this with you and was told you did not verify the correct information.

I am requesting you immediately contact the credit reporting agency with the correct information regarding this account. Please provide me with a copy of the correspondence correcting this. I am prepared to enforce my rights under the Fair Credit Report Act if you do not report the correct information to this agency(s).

Sincerely,

Letter Proposing Settlement

[your name and address]

[name and address of the credit report agency]

[date]

To Whom it May Concern:

With regard to account #_____, which I do not acknowledge to be a debt that I owe, I make the following settlement offer in order to conclude this matter as swiftly as possible. This not a renewed promise to pay and it is not an agreement unless you sign it and return it or we mutually sign a written agreement document. I maintain my right to seek further proof of this debt.

I will pay you_____ in full satisfaction of this debt. Upon receipt of the payment, your company will report this debt to all three major credit report agencies (Equifax, Experian, and TransUnion) as "paid as agreed" and you will remove all references to delinquency on this account. As the company reporting the status of this account, you have full authority to change the way it is listed with credit agencies.

This is a restricted offer. If you agree, sign and return this letter and I will send payment by certified mail. The terms of this offer are confidential. I will make no payment without a written agreement.

Sincerely,

ABOUT THE AUTHOR

Born in Charleston, SC, as a daughter of a naval office, real estate consultant, Shakeima Clark Chatman split her childhood between Charleston and Virginia Beach, Virginia. After high school, she attended South Carolina State University where she majored in Elementary Education. In her professional career, Shakeima has served in several roles in education, corporate training, and software consulting before starting her real estate career. As the owner of The Chatman Group, her mission is to make the American Dream a reality for all individuals. Her real estate career also affords her the flexibility to develop and nurture her true passion and vision: mentoring teenage girls through her nonprofit organization, D.I.V.A.S In Training whose mission is to bring out the moral excellence in teenage girls so that they can aspire for success, power and honor.

Recognized as a REALTOR® of Distinction by her local real estate board, Shakeima is a member of the South Carolina Trident Association of Realtors and the National Association of Realtors. Possessing the Accredited Buyer Representative Designation and the Military Relocation Professional Certification, distinguishes her as a real estate consultant and not just a real estate sales agent. Each week she provides the community with information on the real estate market as the host of her radio show, Possess the Land, featured on Kinetic HiFi, a local, online talk radio station based in Charleston, South Carolina.

A member of Royal Missionary Baptist Church in North Charleston, South Carolina, she volunteers with The Royal Foundation, serving on the Board of Directors and teaches the teens class in the church's youth church services. Her volunteer commitments have included serving as the President for the Jenkins Institute for Children's Advisory Board and serving as a member of the Virginia College Business Advisory Board. Shakeima shares her life with her husband, Andre Chatman and their daughter, Kendyl.

www.ingramcontent.com/pod-product-compliance
Lightning Source LLC
LaVergne TN
LVHW041634070426
835507LV00008B/609